Cameron Mackintosh Presents
Boublil and Schönberg's

ALTO SAXOPHONE

Selections From

Les Misérables™

A Musical by
Alain Boublil & Claude-Michel Schönberg

Lyrics by Herbert Kretzmer

based on the novel by VICTOR HUGO

Music by CLAUDE-MICHEL SCHÖNBERG
Lyrics by HERBERT KRETZMER
Original French text by ALAIN BOUBLIL
and JEAN-MARC NATEL
Additional material by JAMES FENTON

Orchestral score by JOHN CAMERON
Production Musical Supervisor ROBERT BILLIG
Musical Director JAMES MAY
Sound by ANDREW BRUCE/AUTOGRAPH

Associate Director and Executive Producer
RICHARD JAY-ALEXANDER
Executive Producer MARTIN McCALLUM
Casting by JOHNSON-LIFF & ZERMAN
General Management ALAN WASSER

Designed by JOHN NAPIER
Lighting by DAVID HERSEY
Costumes by ANDREANE NEOFITOU

Directed and Adapted by
TREVOR NUNN & JOHN CAIRD

THE MUSICAL SENSATION
1987 TONY® AWARD BEST MUSICAL

CONTENTS

ISBN 978-0-7935-4898-9

This edition Copyright © 1995 by Alain Boublil Music Ltd. (ASCAP)
c/o Stephen Tenenbaum & Co., Inc., 1775 Broadway, Suite 708, New York, NY 10019 Tel. (212) 246-7204, Fax (212) 246-7217
All songs sub-published for the UK and Eire by Alain Boublil (Overseas) Ltd. (PRS), 9 Collingham Gardens, London, England SW5 0HS

ALAIN BOUBLIL MUSIC LTD.

EXCLUSIVELY DISTRIBUTED BY

777 W. BLUEMOUND RD. P.O. BOX 13819 MILWAUKEE, WI 53213

Visit Hal Leonard Online at
www.halleonard.com

AT THE END OF THE DAY

Alto Saxophone

Music by CLAUDE-MICHEL SCHÖNBERG
Lyrics by HERBERT KRETZMER
Original Text by ALAIN BOUBLIL and JEAN-MARC NATEL

BRING HIM HOME

Alto Saxophone

Music by CLAUDE-MICHEL SCHÖNBERG
Lyrics by HERBERT KRETZMER and ALAIN BOUBLIL

CASTLE ON A CLOUD

Alto Saxophone

Music by CLAUDE-MICHEL SCHÖNBERG
Lyrics by HERBERT KRETZMER
Original Text by ALAIN BOUBLIL and JEAN-MARC NATEL

DO YOU HEAR THE PEOPLE SING?

Alto Saxophone

Music by CLAUDE-MICHEL SCHÖNBERG
Lyrics by HERBERT KRETZMER
Original Text by ALAIN BOUBLIL and JEAN-MARC NATEL

DRINK WITH ME

(To Days Gone By)

Alto Saxophone

Music by CLAUDE-MICHEL SCHÖNBERG
Lyrics by HERBERT KRETZMER and ALAIN BOUBLIL

EMPTY CHAIRS AT EMPTY TABLES

Alto Saxophone

Music by CLAUDE-MICHEL SCHÖNBERG
Lyrics by HERBERT KRETZMER and ALAIN BOUBLIL

Music and Lyrics Copyright © 1986 by Alain Boublil Ltd. (ASCAP)
This edition Copyright © 1995 by Alain Boublil Music Ltd. (ASCAP)
Mechanical and Publication Rights for the U.S.A. Administered by Alain Boublil Music Ltd. (ASCAP)
c/o Stephen Tenenbaum & Co., Inc., 1775 Broadway, Suite 708, New York, NY 10019, Tel. (212) 246-7204, Fax (212) 246-7217
International Copyright Secured.   All Rights Reserved.   This music is copyright.   Photocopying is illegal.
All Performance Rights Restricted.

A HEART FULL OF LOVE

Alto Saxophone

Music by CLAUDE-MICHEL SCHÖNBERG
Lyrics by HERBERT KRETZMER
Original Text by ALAIN BOUBLIL and JEAN-MARC NATEL

poco rall.

meno mosso

rall.

I DREAMED A DREAM

Alto Saxophone

Music by CLAUDE-MICHEL SCHÖNBERG
Lyrics by HERBERT KRETZMER
Original Text by ALAIN BOUBLIL and JEAN-MARC NATEL

IN MY LIFE

Alto Saxophone

Music by CLAUDE-MICHEL SCHÖNBERG
Lyrics by HERBERT KRETZMER
Original Text by ALAIN BOUBLIL and JEAN-MARC NATEL

A LITTLE FALL OF RAIN

Alto Saxophone

Music by CLAUDE-MICHEL SCHÖNBERG
Lyrics by HERBERT KRETZMER
Original Text by ALAIN BOUBLIL and JEAN-MARC NATEL

ON MY OWN

Alto Saxophone

Music by CLAUDE-MICHEL SCHÖNBERG
Lyrics by ALAIN BOUBLIL, HERBERT KRETZMER, JOHN CAIRD,
TREVOR NUNN and JEAN-MARC NATEL

STARS

Alto Saxophone

Music by CLAUDE-MICHEL SCHÖNBERG
Lyrics by HERBERT KRETZMER and ALAIN BOUBLIL

WHO AM I?

Alto Saxophone

Music by CLAUDE-MICHEL SCHÖNBERG
Lyrics by HERBERT KRETZMER
Original Text by ALAIN BOUBLIL and JEAN-MARC NATEL

Enjoy Playing Great Hit Songs on Piano Now with Music from Your Favorite
CLASSIC & CONTEMPORARY ARTISTS

Order these and many more easy piano songbooks from Hal Leonard

ABBA – GOLD
00306820 19 songs $19.99

ADELE – 21
00307320 11 songs $19.99

ADELE – 25
00155394 11 songs $16.99

THE BEATLES – 1
00307219 27 songs $17.99

THE BEATLES BEST
00231944 120 songs $24.99

THE BEATLES GREATEST HITS
00490364 25 songs $19.99

THE BEATLES – LIVE AT THE HOLLYWOOD BOWL
00202248 16 songs $14.99

BEST OF JUSTIN BIEBER
00248635 12 songs $14.99

BEST OF MICHAEL BUBLÉ
00307144 14 songs $16.99

BEST OF CARPENTERS
00306427 18 songs $19.99

BEST OF CHICAGO
00306536 16 songs $19.99

ERIC CLAPTON COLLECTION
00277346 11 songs $14.99

BEST OF COLDPLAY
00306560 16 songs $16.99

BOB DYLAN
14041363 13 songs $16.99

EAGLES GREATEST HITS
00293339 10 songs $14.99

BILLIE EILISH – DON'T SMILE AT ME
00323125 10 songs $19.99

BILLIE EILISH – WHEN WE ALL FALL ASLEEP WHERE DO WE GO?
00323126 13 songs $19.99

BEST OF FLEETWOOD MAC
00109467 12 songs $19.99

ARIANA GRANDE
00293337 14 songs $19.99

GRATEFUL DEAD
00139463 12 songs $19.99

IMAGINE DRAGONS
00294441 14 songs $19.99

MICHAEL JACKSON NUMBER ONES
00322301 18 songs $19.99

BILLY JOEL
00356295 21 songs $19.99

BEST OF BILLY JOEL
00110007 21 songs $19.99

ELTON JOHN ANTHOLOGY
00357102 30 songs $19.99

ELTON JOHN GREATEST HITS
00222538 17 songs $16.99

BEST OF NORAH JONES
00354465 14 songs $19.99

CAROLE KING – TAPESTRY
00306555 12 songs $17.99

LADY GAGA – THE FAME
00307182 14 songs $14.99

LADY GAGA – THE FAME MONSTER
00307181 8 songs $19.99

BEST OF JOHN LEGEND
00224732 14 songs $19.99

THE LUMINEERS
00334067 15 songs $17.99

BOB MARLEY
00129927 14 songs $17.99

MAROON 5
00152665 13 songs $14.99

BEST OF BRUNO MARS
00221887 11 songs $16.99

KACEY MUSGRAVES – GOLDEN HOUR
00350622 13 songs $19.99

KATY PERRY
00248632 12 songs $16.99

THE PIANO GUYS – SIMPLIFIED FAVORITES, VOL. 1
00127421 12 songs $19.99

THE PIANO GUYS – SIMPLIFIED FAVORITES, VOL. 2
00234609 14 songs $19.99

ELVIS PRESLEY – GREATEST HITS
00308205 27 songs $17.99

PRINCE – ULTIMATE
00302630 28 songs $22.99

QUEEN COLLECTION
00139187 10 songs $17.99

BEST OF ED SHEERAN
00236098 14 songs $19.99

SAM SMITH – THE THRILL OF IT ALL
00257747 14 songs $17.99

TAYLOR SWIFT ANTHOLOGY
00254846 20 songs $24.99

TAYLOR SWIFT – EVERMORE
00363715 17 songs $22.99

TAYLOR SWIFT – FEARLESS
00307060 13 songs $16.99

TAYLOR SWIFT – FOLKLORE
00356888 17 songs $19.99

TAYLOR SWIFT – LOVER
00322685 18 songs $19.99

U2 – 18 SINGLES
00307285 18 songs $19.99

STEVIE WONDER ANTHOLOGY
00306258 27 songs $19.99

HAL•LEONARD®

www.halleonard.com

Prices, contents, and availability subject to change without notice.

0221
332